Space Research
How Does It Affect Life on Earth?

BTR Zone (Bridge to Reading) is published by Capstone Classroom, 1710 Roe Crest Drive, North Mankato, Minnesota 56003 www.capstoneclassroom.com

ISBN: 978-1-62521-036-4

Editorial Credits
Christopher L. Harbo, editor; Kyle Grenz, cover designer; Kazuko Collins, layout artist; Eric Gohl, media researcher

Photo Credits
Dreamstime: Walter Arce, 43; iStockphotos: Claudia Dewald, 16 (back); Landov: Reuters, 30; NASA: cover, 4, 7, 9, 12, 16 (front), 36, David Higginbotham, 35, LANCE Rapid Response/Jeff Schmaltz, 24, Robert Markowitz, 11; NOAA: 20; Shutterstock: Brian L. Hendricks, 26, BW Folsom, 19, epstock, 33, maiwharn, 14, Thomas M Perkins, 28, Viappy, 40; Wikipedia: Agência Brasil/Valter Campanato, 39, Filya1, 17, Gobierno de Chile, 23

Design Elements: Shutterstock

About the Cover
NASA astronaut Steve Bowen works on construction and maintenance of the *International Space Station* during a space walk on May 17, 2010.

TABLE OF CONTENTS

Astronaut Edwin "Buzz" Aldrin walks on the moon in 1969.

CHAPTER 1

NASA, America's Space Agency

What does the word **NASA** mean to you? Do you think of spaceships? What about **astronauts**? These things are part of NASA. But NASA also makes products to improve our lives.

NASA formed in 1958 with a plan to explore outer space. In 1969 NASA landed a spaceship on the moon. In the 1970s, NASA sent spaceships to study the planet Mars. Through the years, NASA learned a lot about the sun and planets. It built products to make better spaceships and space suits. Soon people found a way to use these products on Earth. These new products are called **spin-offs**. You use many of them almost every day.

NASA · short for National Aeronautics and Space Administration

astronaut · a person who is trained to live and work in space

spin-off · a product made for public use, based on an earlier model

5

Everyday Products

You wake up in the morning. You stretch out on a foam mattress. How's the weather? You check it on a TV that gets information from a **satellite**, or spacecraft, that circles Earth. In the kitchen, you grab some freeze-dried berries. You put on your sunglasses. The lenses have a special coating. Your eyes are safe from the sun's rays. You can thank space research for these cool products. These discoveries came from the space program!

NASA Programs

These are some of NASA's programs. Each program teaches scientists a lot about Earth and space.

satellite · a spacecraft that circles Earth, another planet, or some object in space

Two astronauts make repairs to the *International Space Station (ISS)*.

Space Shuttle

NASA launched the first of six space shuttles in 1981. These spacecraft flew like spaceships but landed like airplanes. Each one flew many times. There were 135 flights in all. Astronauts lived on the shuttles. They helped build the *International Space Station (ISS)*. The last space shuttle flew in 2011.

International Space Station

The *ISS* was put together in space. People live and work there. They study how space affects our bodies. Some astronauts do **space walks** outside of the *ISS*. They wear space suits. Sometimes you can see the *ISS* in the night sky. It looks like a moving ball of light.

Satellites

More than 2,500 satellites circle Earth. Some track the weather. Others send messages to Earth. Do you use a cell phone? Do you use the **Internet** on a computer? They could not work without messages from satellites. Some satellites help us learn about other planets and stars.

Hubble

Scientists use a tool called the Hubble Space **Telescope**. A telescope helps people look at stars and planets. Hubble was carried into space by the space shuttle in 1990. Scientists use Hubble to look deep into space.

space walk · a period of time during which an astronaut leaves the spacecraft to move around in space

Internet · a system that allows people to share information with others through computers

telescope · a tool people use to look at objects in space

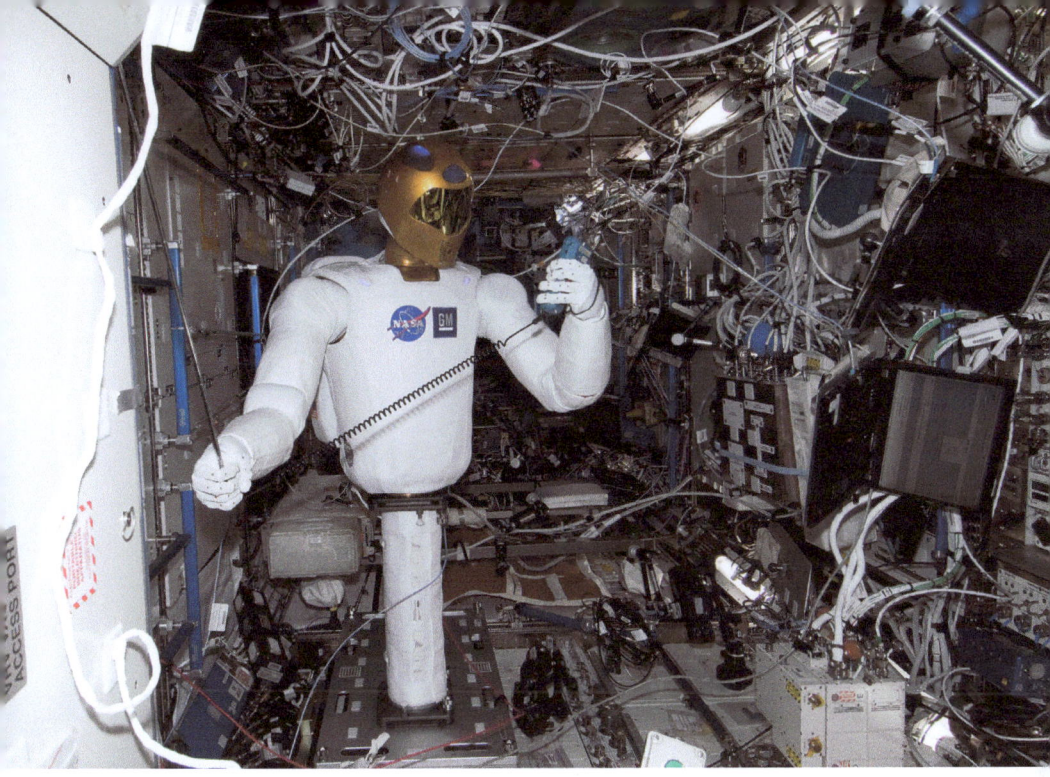

Robonaut 2 holds an instrument that measures air speed on the *ISS*.

Meet Robonaut!

Some jobs are too dangerous for astronauts. Robonaut 2 (R2) helps them on the *ISS*. R2 moves its arms and hands like a person. It flips switches and turns knobs. It can turn its head.

People control R2's movements. Cameras in R2's eyes let the controller see. The controller wears special gloves to move R2's hands. A helmet lets the controller move R2's head. Soon R2 will get legs and feet. It will move around the *ISS* on its own. Space walks for R2 are being planned. R2 won't need a space suit.

Mars Landing

Some satellites circle the planet Mars. They send back **data**, or information. NASA has also landed spacecraft on Mars. **Rovers** are robots that drive on Mars. They take soil samples. They look for water. Can we live there? We may find out someday soon!

The X1 Exoskeleton

X1 is a spin-off from Robonaut 2. It is not in use yet, but it will be soon. X1 is worn over a person's body. Motors make it work. X1 can turn, step, and point.

Astronauts feel **weightless** and float on the *ISS*. It is hard to stay fit. Astronauts use a treadmill. Soon they may use X1 instead. They would put X1 on. The joints would be locked. By moving against the joints, astronauts' muscles would stay strong.

data · information or facts
rover · a robot used to explore objects in space
weightless · free of the feeling of gravity

The X1 exoskeleton will one day help astronauts keep their muscles strong in space.

Dextre is used to move cargo outside the *ISS*.

Dextre

The *ISS* also has a robot called Dextre. Its body has two arms and no head. Dextre's hands look like big claws. The Canadian Space Agency (CSA) created Dextre. The CSA and NASA work together to use it.

Spaceships bring **cargo**, or supplies, to the *ISS*. A person on Earth controls Dextre to unpack the cargo. The robot puts it on the *ISS*. Dextre can even work while astronauts sleep. It saves a lot of time for astronauts.

cargo · things sent by space shuttles or other spacecraft

CHAPTER 2

Sensational Spin-offs

You've already read about some of NASA's programs. Now let's find out more about its exciting spin-offs.

A Bounce in Your Step

Some shoes feel soft and bouncy. You can walk or stand for a long time. That's because the bottom of these shoes are made of foam. The foam protects your feet and legs.

In the late 1960s, astronauts walked on the moon for the first time. The ground was hard and rocky. The astronauts needed special boots. These boots helped them bounce when they walked. Foam was part of the boots. Soon shoe companies began using the same foam.

Shoe companies began using foam in shoes after NASA used it for astronauts' boots.

Look at Those Eyes

Astronauts wear helmets in space. The helmets have clear visors so they can see. There's a lot of dirt and dust in space. It gets on the visors. The astronauts had trouble seeing. NASA needed a way to protect the visors. They invented plastic coating.

Can you guess how plastic coating helps people on Earth? Look at a pair of glasses. Some lenses are made of plastic. The plastic scratches easily. But many lenses have a special coating. The coating stops the scratches. People can see where they are going. The coating also protects their eyes from the sun.

visor

NASA developed a special coating that protects many glasses from scratches.

The sensor created for NASA now helps nearly every cell phone take pictures.

Take a Picture

Spacecraft need cameras. They take pictures of space and other planets. The cameras used to be big. The pictures were not always clear. Dr. Eric R. Fossum invented a special **sensor** in the 1990s. It lets small cameras take clear pictures. The sensor is one of NASA's most-used spin-offs. It helps cell phones take pictures. The sensor can also be placed into a tiny camera that can fit inside a pill. When the pill is swallowed, the camera takes pictures. It sends pictures to a computer. Doctors use these pictures to save lives.

sensor · an instrument that can see changes and send the information to another device

Clean Water

People need clean drinking water. If they drink dirty water, they might get sick. Special **filters** clean the water. The water goes through the filter. Charcoal and other materials in the filter clean the water.

Filters have been around since the 1950s. But NASA made them better. In space, there is no water. Spaceship and *ISS* crews bring the water with them. It is hard to keep the water clean. NASA filters clean the water. Astronauts can reuse water and not get sick when they drink it.

Freeze-dried Food

Space crews can't take enough fresh food to last their whole time in space. So NASA developed a freeze-drying process. First food is cooked. Next it is frozen. Then the water is sucked out. The food lasts for years. Freeze-dried foods are light and small.

Freeze-dried food looks almost like regular food. But it's dry instead of moist. To eat it, just add water and stir. Campers and soldiers use it. You might want to try some freeze-dried fruits.

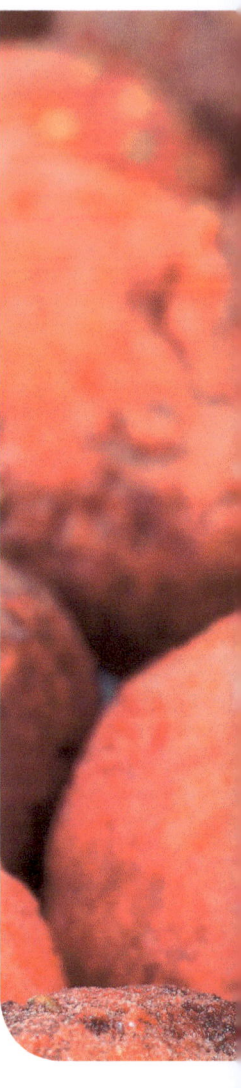

Freeze-dried strawberries are dry and crunchy after their water is removed.

filter · a device that cleans liquids or gases as they pass through it

A satellite picture shows the line of thunderstorms that swept over Joplin, Missouri, in 2011.

atmosphere · the layer of gases that surrounds Earth

tornado · a whirling column of air that stretches from a thunderstorm to the ground

CHAPTER 3

Public Safety

Many space-age products are handy. But some save lives too. Many spin-offs help safety workers do their jobs better.

Tracking Storms

Some satellites have circled Earth for more than 20 years. They take pictures of storms in the **atmosphere**, or layer of gases, around Earth. They measure wind speed. They track the amount of rain. Scientists learn more about storms.

In 2011 a **tornado** struck in the state of Missouri. The tornado came from a line of strong thunderstorms. The GOES-13 satellite took pictures of the storms. The pictures helped scientists learn more about tornadoes.

NASA's HS3 program studies hurricanes. The program uses planes called Global Hawks. These planes don't need pilots. The planes fly above the storms. They collect weather data. Scientists study the data. They learn how the hurricanes form.

Search and Rescue

During storms, there can be floods. It's hard for rescue crews to find people. NASA satellites help. Satellite data goes to computers. The computers make maps and charts of a place. Where are the people? How deep is the water? Crews know the answers. They can work quickly to save lives.

In 2010 a group of miners in the country of Chile got stuck 2,300 feet (700 meters) under the ground. A NASA crew helped with the rescue. They went to the **mine**, or place where workers dig underground. They helped design a capsule called Fénix. The capsule was sent into the ground. The miners came up in it one at a time. All of them lived.

In the Planning Stages

NASA is working on a new rescue system. It will have instruments on satellites. They will look for emergency **beacons**. Beacons may be on ships or airplanes. A beacon gives out a signal. The instruments read the signal. They find the beacon. Rescuers can then find the people who used the beacon.

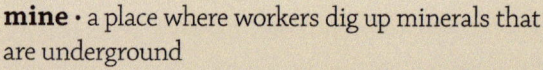

mine · a place where workers dig up minerals that are underground

beacon · a small radio that sends out information

NASA helped design the Fénix capsule used to rescue miners in Chile in 2010.

When planes crash, they may be hard to find. NASA thinks **Laser** Search and Rescue (L-SAR) may help. A laser is a thin stream of light. How does L-SAR work? A vehicle has special tape on it. The tape reflects light. A laser on an airplane reads the light. It tells the search crew where to look.

laser · a thin stream of light with a lot of energy

A GFIMS picture shows wisps of smoke coming from fires in central Russia in 2012.

Detecting Forest Fires

Forest fires are a big danger around the world. About 865 million acres (350 million hectares) of land catch fire each year. NASA developed the Global Fire Information Management System (GFIMS) to help.

GFIMS works from a satellite. It watches forests and fields. Is there a hot spot? This is a place where a fire might start. GFIMS will find it. GFIMS will find ongoing fires too. Then GFIMS sends e-mails to a control center. It sends pictures. The crews know how to plan. They can alert people near the fires and save lives.

Meet MARSHA

MARSHA is a robot. Its name stands for Mobile and Remote Sensing Hazmat Activity. MARSHA is wireless. A person controls it from a distance. MARSHA is used when there is a danger to people. Rescue teams send MARSHA in first. The robot's sensors see, smell, and hear what is going on. It sends data to the rescue team. The team can make a plan. They know how many people they need to send. They know what equipment to use.

Firefighters use breathing gear that was first developed for NASA astronauts.

Protecting Firefighters

Rocket motors get hot. They need to be protected. NASA made special paint and foam. They resist heat and fire. Now firefighters' tools are coated with the paint and foam. NASA also made fabrics that resist fire. Some clothes are now made

with this fabric.

cylinder

NASA designed breathing gear for moon landings. Astronauts wore a special face mask. They also carried **cylinders** on their backs. Each cylinder had 30 minutes of air in it. It was lightweight. A beep warned when the air was running out.

In 1975 the New York City Fire Department started using the breathing gear. Rescuers had fewer injuries from breathing smoke. Fire departments all over the country use the gear today.

cylinder · a tube with circular sides

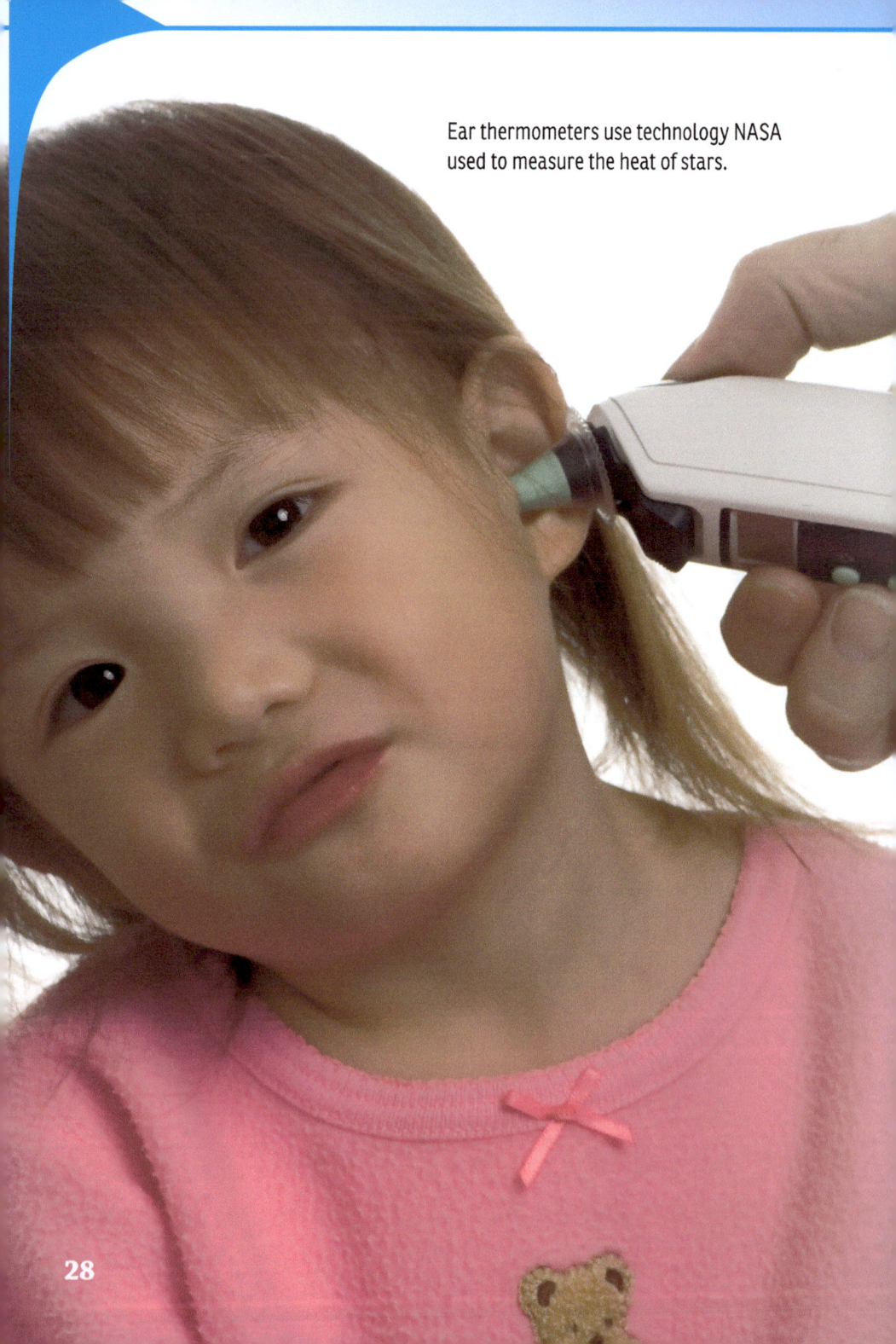

Ear thermometers use technology NASA used to measure the heat of stars.

CHAPTER 4

Health and Medicine

Health and medicine always need to improve. NASA's space-age technology helps saves lives.

A Quick Reading

Have you ever taken your own temperature? You probably put a **thermometer** under your tongue. Then you waited a while. You had to stay still. An ear thermometer works much faster. Hold one end. Place the other end just inside the ear. It measures the heat inside the ear. In seconds the temperature reading appears.

NASA first used this technology to measure the heat of stars and planets. Doctors and nurses now use this technology all the time. It saves time and lives.

thermometer · a tool that measures temperature

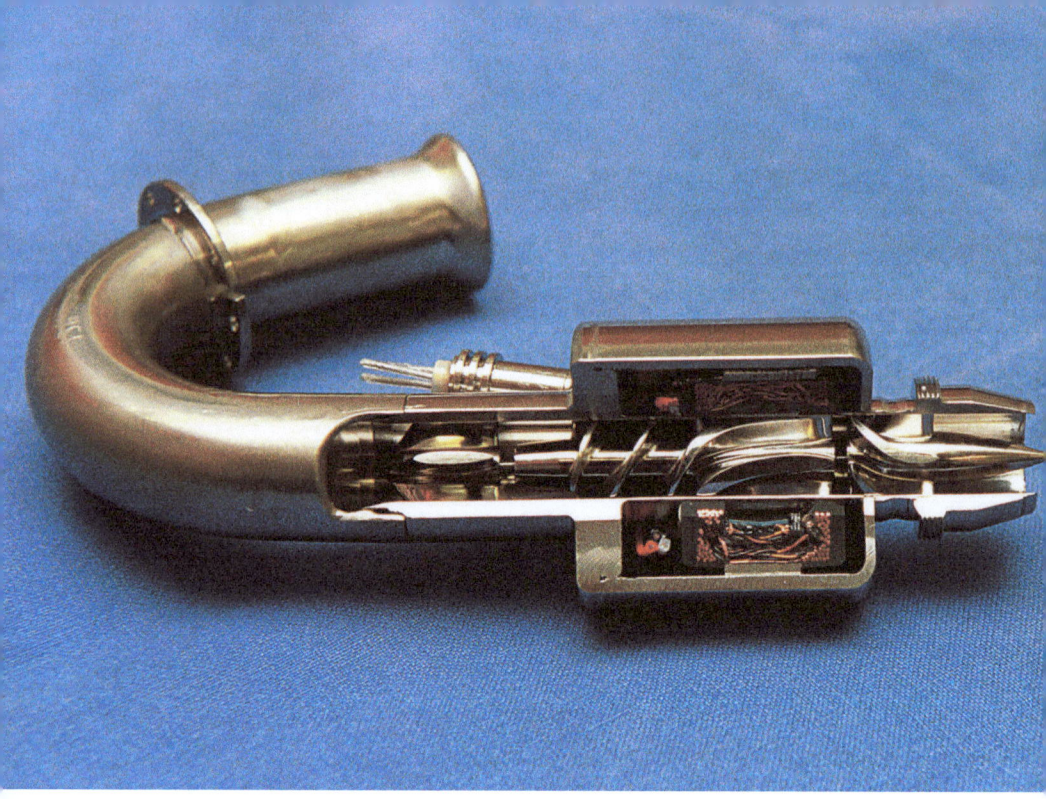

Dr. Michael DeBakey's heart pump got its start as a NASA fuel pump.

Keeping Hearts Pumping

Many people have heart problems. Sometimes a heart cannot correctly pump blood. This is dangerous. Once again a NASA product was a big help. NASA makes tiny devices for spacecraft. Doctors used NASA's ideas to make a machine called AICD. It goes inside the chest near the heart. Doctors attach special wires to the heart. These wires measure heartbeats. When the heart does not beat correctly, electricity is sent to the heart. The heart then beats correctly again.

Tiny Heart Pump

Dr. Michael DeBakey was a heart doctor.
He knew some people have hearts that don't
work well. Some people need to get a new heart.
DeBakey worked with NASA. The space shuttle
engines used fuel pumps. Together NASA and
DeBakey developed a tiny pump. The pump fits
inside a human heart. The pump helps blood flow
smoothly. Sometimes people can keep using
the pump. Then they don't need a new heart.
The heart pump has saved hundreds of lives.
It's one of NASA's most helpful spin-offs.

Look Closely

NASA satellites use **scanners**. A scanner is a machine that takes pictures. Some scanners look at large objects. Others look at tiny details. One type is called a CT scanner. Another is an MRI.

Doctors also need clear pictures. They use the technology from NASA scanners. Their scanners look inside the human body. Some look for damaged body parts. One scanner looks inside the heart.

The scanners save lives. They find cancer and other diseases early. This helps doctors give better treatment.

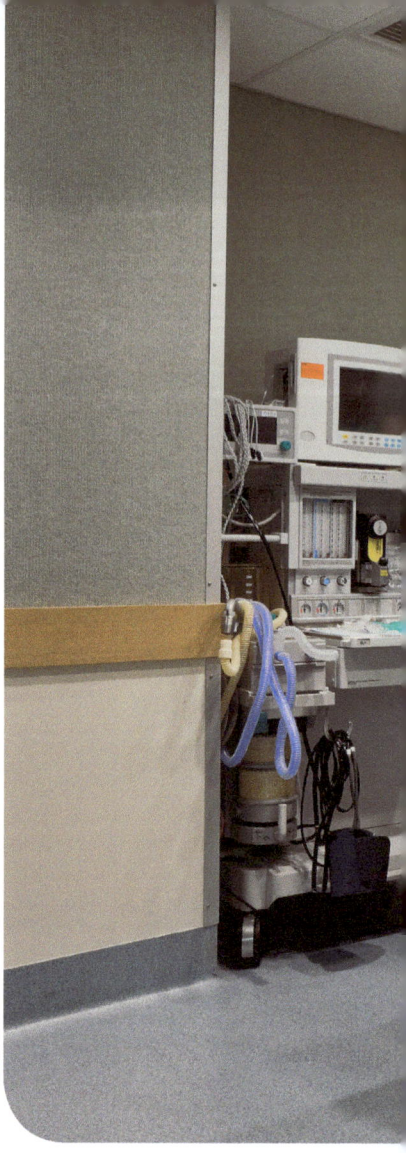

scanner · a machine that takes pictures

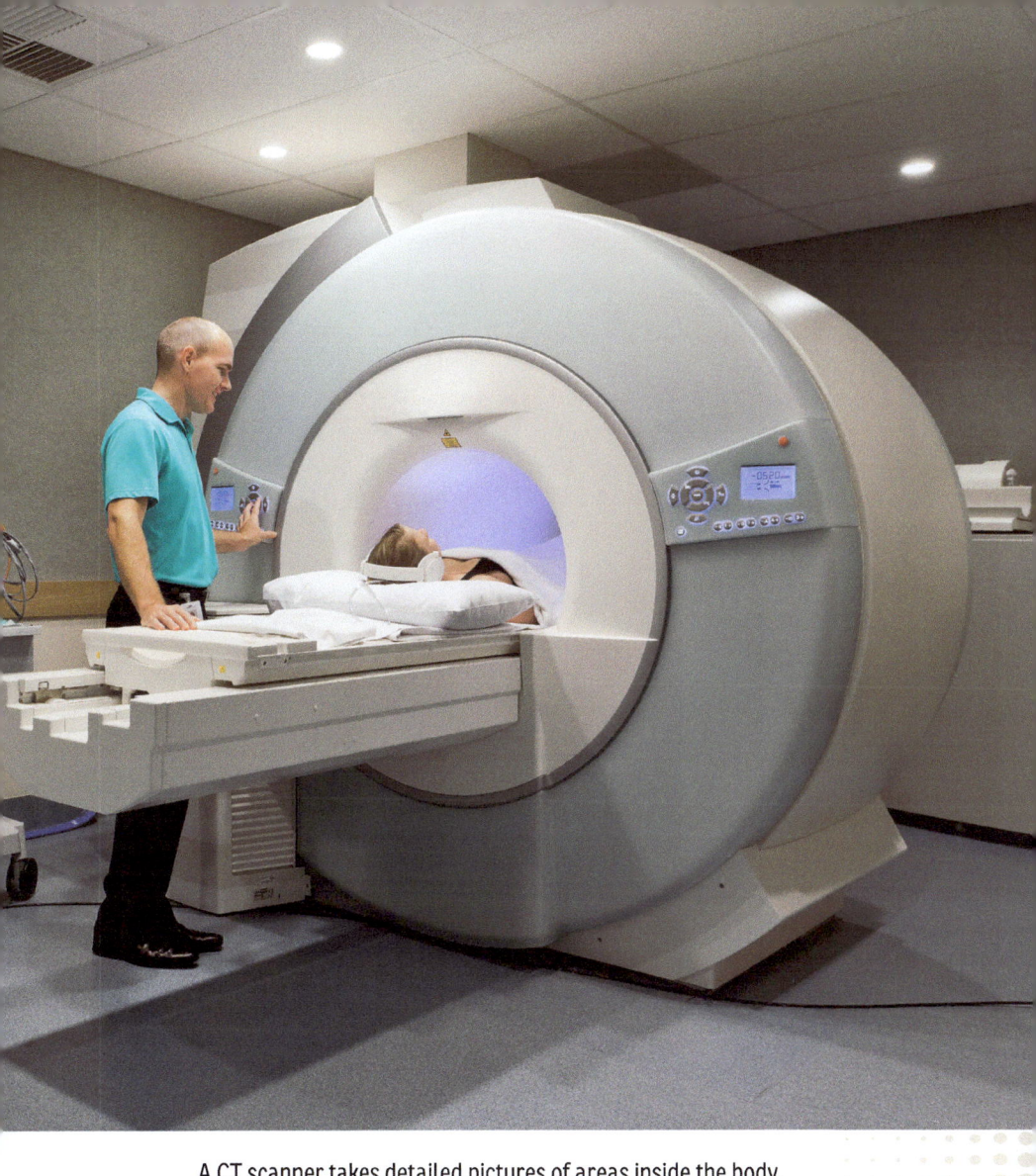

A CT scanner takes detailed pictures of areas inside the body.

Light to Heal and Save

The space shuttle crews did experiments with plants. What kinds of lights did plants need? The crews used **LEDs**. These tiny lights worked well. They made the plants grow.

Doctors started to use the LEDs. They learned that LEDs can kill cancer. Cancer can form a tumor, or lump. Doctors used LEDs to help destroy the tumor. An LED can work for many hours. It does not get hot. The rest of the body stays safe.

Laser Treatments

Without space research we might not have laser treatments. Lasers are used to treat wounds. Two tools are called the WARP 10 and the WARP 75. They were made for soldiers in battle. You hold them in your hand. The WARP 10 and WARP 75 work quickly. Light goes into the muscles and heals them. The tools stay cool and are easy to use.

LED · short for Light Emitting Diode, a device that sends out light

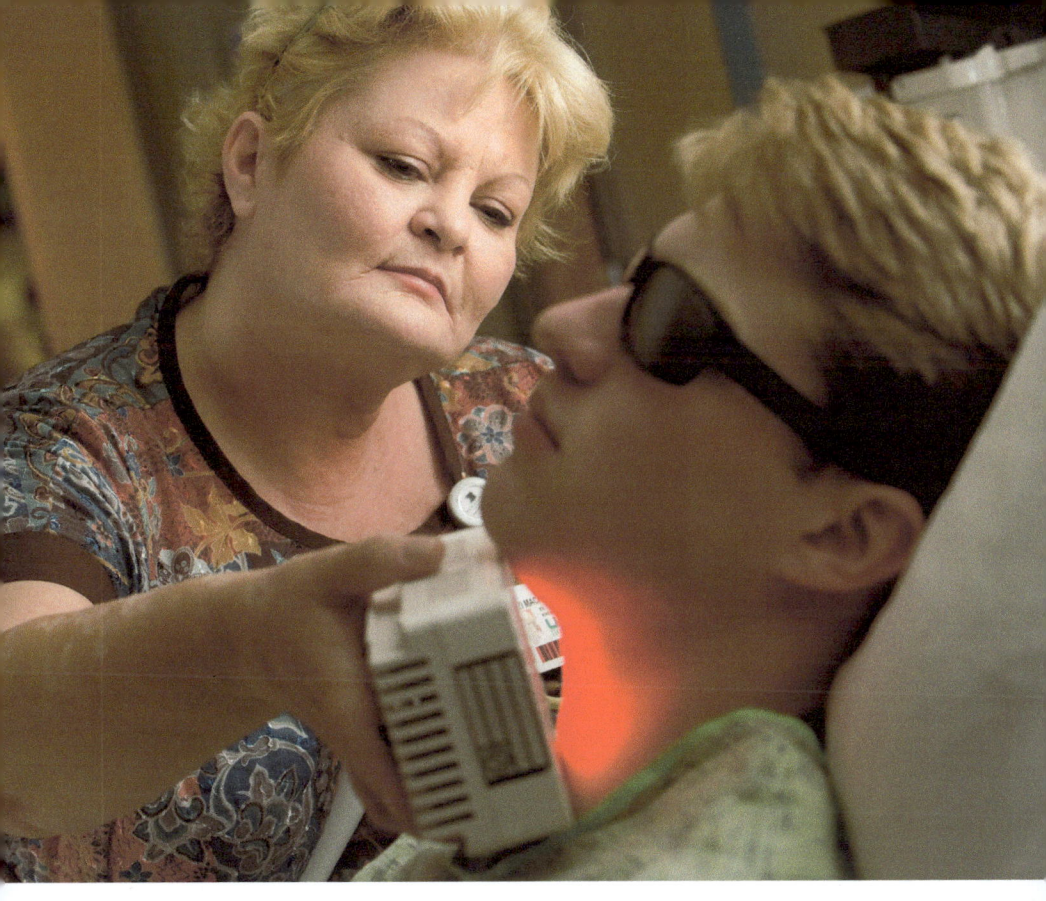

A nurse uses a WARP 75 laser to treat a patient.

Eye surgery used to be very risky. LASIK surgery is much safer. Lasers are used to fix eye problems. The doctor puts a laser on the eye. When the eyes heal, most people no longer need glasses.

NASA's Quiet Aircraft Technology Program (QATP) tests a model aircraft in a wind tunnel.

Transportation

NASA develops new technology for spaceships. A lot of the spin-offs help improve vehicles and airplanes on Earth.

Shhh, Quiet

Noisy airplane engines are a problem. People in the plane hear the noise. People on the ground hear it too. NASA's Quiet Aircraft Technology Program (QATP) is trying to help.

The QATP team studies airplane engines and bodies. They find out where the noise comes from. They test new engines and wings. These engines and wings make less noise.

The team also studies noise from engine **exhaust**. This is the hot air and gases that leaves the engine. It mixes with cold air and makes noise. The team put new parts on the engines. Now the air comes out in a different place. Less noise is created.

exhaust · the hot air and gases that leave an engine

Grooved Runways

Airplane tires used to skid and slide on runways wet with rain. Wet runways sometimes caused planes to crash. In the 1960s, scientists at NASA had an idea. They cut grooves across the runway. The water went into the grooves. It flowed away from the runway. Airports all over the world started making grooved runways.

NASA told highway departments about the runways. Soon, grooves were cut into many roads. The state of California studied some streets before and after putting in the grooves. There were 85 percent fewer accidents after the grooves were cut.

NASA added the grooves in runways to make them safer for landings on rainy days.

Hybrids

Most spacecraft get power in more than one way. They may use batteries or fuel. They use power from the sun. All of the types of power work together.

An electric car plugs into an outlet to recharge its battery.

Right now, most cars run only on gas. But there are some new **hybrid** cars. These cars use more than one type of fuel. NASA and its partners are working on new systems for hybrid cars. They may use batteries and fuel. The cars will run better. They will use less gas.

Can we change old cars into hybrid cars? NASA and its partners think so. This process will save people a lot of money. They will not have to buy new hybrid cars or trucks.

hybrid · a mix of two different types; hybrid engines run on electricity and gasoline or diesel fuel

41

More NASA Spin-offs

SPIN-OFF: Normal home ovens heat the air around the food. NASA invented a way to have hot air blown directly on food. By heating the food directly, the food cooks faster.

SPIN-OFF: NASA invented a special video headset. Scientists used it when they needed to work with clearer pictures. Now people with poor vision use it. These people can now watch TV and read more easily.

SPIN-OFF: Cordless technology was used first by NASA. The next time you are talking on a cordless phone, you can thank NASA.

SPIN-OFF: NASA invented material to protect space vehicles against very high temperatures. NASCAR now uses this material to protect race car drivers from the high heat of their cars' engines.

SPIN-OFF: A material NASA designed for the *ISS* is helping golfers. A company created golf clubs using this new metal material. It gives golfers more spin on the ball.

Race car driver suits use the same technology as astronaut suits to make them heat resistant.

SPIN-OFF: Tracking devices used on space shuttle missions now help track vehicles on Earth. Next time your parents use a GPS to find their way home, remember NASA used it first.

Read More

Kortenkamp, Steve. *Space Robots.* Incredible Space. Mankato, Minn.: Capstone Press, 2009.

Morris, Neil. *What Does Space Exploration Do for Us?* Earth, Space, and Beyond. Chicago: Raintree, 2012.

Rooney, Anne. *Outer Space.* Earth's Final Frontiers. Chicago: Heinemann Library, 2008.

Tagliaferro, Linda. *Who Walks in Space?: Working In Space.* Wild Work. Chicago: Raintree, 2011.

Internet Sites

FactHound offers a safe, fun way to find Internet sites related to this book. All of the sites on FactHound have been researched by our staff.

Here's all you do:
Visit *www.facthound.com*
Type in this code: 9781625210364

Check out projects, games and lots more at
www.capstonekids.com

Glossary
of Text Features

Text Feature	How to Use It
Caption: A word or group of words shown with a picture or illustration	Read a caption to understand information that may not be in the text.
Diagram: A drawing that shows or explains something	Examine a diagram to understand steps in a process, how something is made, or the parts of something.
Glossary: List of key terms with their meanings	Look up key terms in the glossary to find their meanings and to get a better understanding of the topic of the text.
Index: Alphabetical list of key terms, names, and topics in a text with their page numbers	Use the index to find pages that contain information you are looking for.
Map: A drawing that represents a place, such as a country or city	Use a map to understand relative locations and determine where events took place.
Photograph or Illustration: Visuals that are created by cameras or drawn	Examine photographs and illustrations to better understand ideas in the text that might be unclear.
Subhead: Word or group of words that divides the text into sections and tells the main idea of a section	Use subheads to locate information in the text and understand how a text is organized.
Table: Represents data in a small space	Examine a table to understand data or to compare information in the text.
Table of Contents: List of the major parts of the book and their page numbers	Use a table of contents to locate general information in the text and see how the topics are organized.
Text Box: A box in the text that provides extra information about a topic	Read a text box to understand interesting or important information.
Text Style: Bold, color, or italic words in the text	Pay attention to bold, italic, and color words to figure out which words in the text are important.
Timeline: Shows events in the order in which they occurred	Use a timeline to understand the order in which events occurred or how one event led to another.

Glossary

astronaut (AS-truh-nawt) · a person who is trained to live and work in space

atmosphere (AT-muhss-fihr) · the layer of gases that surrounds Earth

beacon (BEE-kuhn) · a small radio that sends out information

cargo (KAHR-goh) · things sent by space shuttles or other spacecraft

cylinder (SI-luhn-duhr) · a tube with circular sides

data (DAY-tuh) · information or facts

exhaust (ig-ZAWST) · the hot air and gases that leave an engine

filter (FIL-tuhr) · a device that cleans liquids or gases as they pass through it

hybrid (HYE-brid) · a mix of two different types; hybrid engines run on electricity and gasoline or diesel fuel

Internet (IN-tur-net) · a system that allows people to share information with others through computers

laser (LAY-zur) · a thin stream of light with a lot of energy

LED (EL-ee-dee) · short for Light Emitting Diode, a device that sends out light

mine (MINE) · a place where workers dig up minerals that are underground

NASA (NA-saw) • short for National Aeronautics and Space Administration; NASA is a U.S. government agency that does research on flight and space exploration

rover (ROH-vur) • a robot used to explore objects in space

satellite (SAT-uh-lite) • a spacecraft that circles Earth, another planet, or some object in space

scanner (SKAN-ur) • a machine that takes pictures

sensor (SEN-sur) • an instrument that can see changes and send the information to another device

space walk (SPAYSS WAWK) • a period of time during which an astronaut leaves the spacecraft to move around in space

spin-off (SPIN AWF) • a product made for public use, based on an earlier model

telescope (TEL-uh-skope) • a tool people use to look at objects in space

thermometer (thur-MOM-uh-tur) • a tool that measures temperature

tornado (tor-NAY-doh) • a whirling column of air that stretches from a thunderstorm to the ground

weightless (WATE-liss) • free of the feeling of gravity

Index

The United States was the first country to land a person on the moon.

NASA Space Programs

NASA was formed in 1958, and the first American satellite was launched that same year. Not long after, NASA's *Mercury* and *Gemini* missions sent astronauts into space. NASA sent humans into space many times before the *Apollo 11* moon mission.

The *Gemini-5* spacecraft launches into space.

American astronauts travelled in small **capsules**. Each of these small vehicles sat on top of a large rocket. The rocket launched the capsule out of Earth's **atmosphere**. Once in outer space, the rocket disconnected (released) from the capsule. The capsule then moved into orbit around Earth. Scientists used computers on Earth to monitor the orbiting capsule. As always, these programs were developed under complete secrecy.

Selecting the First Astronauts

America's first astronauts were chosen from the U.S. military's test pilots. These men had to be smart, healthy, and fairly short. Early space capsules were very small, so being short was a good thing.

capsule · a sealed vehicle in which a person can ride in flight in space

atmosphere · the mixture of gases that surrounds the earth

Life in Space

Getting ahead in the space race meant overcoming many scientific challenges. One of the challenges facing American and Soviet scientists was how astronauts would respond to life in space. Living without **gravity** was one of their biggest concerns. Gravity is the force pulling objects toward Earth's center.

To learn more about how space travel affects living things, scientists sent animals into space. In 1957 the Soviets sent a dog named Laika into space as part of the *Sputnik II* mission. Laika was the first living creature sent into orbit. Information from this mission helped the Soviets successfully send the first human into space.

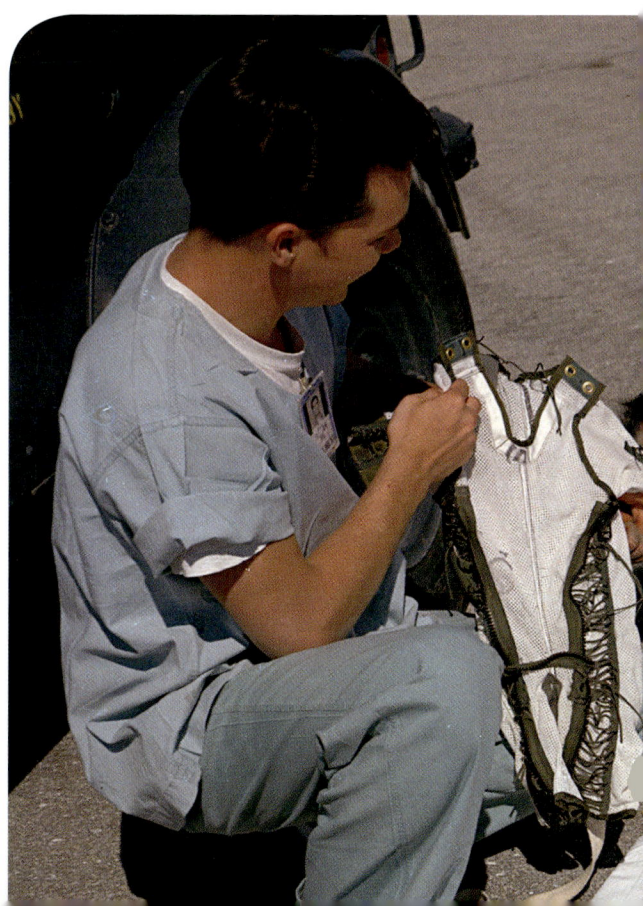

Astrochimps wore tiny spacesuits on their journey into outer space.

In the early 1960s NASA had a crew of trained "astrochimps." These chimpanzees were trained to operate levers inside the space capsule. The animals were sent into space on early *Mercury* missions. Scientists studied how **radiation**, noise, less gravity, vibrations, and other conditions affected them. The astrochimps proved they could operate the levers in these conditions and make it back to Earth safely. They paved the way for American astronauts.

gravity · a force that pulls objects with mass together; gravity pulls objects down toward the center of Earth

radiation · rays of energy given off by certain elements

Mercury 9 was designed to withstand extreme friction.

Fighting Friction

Spacecraft move very fast through space. When spacecraft hit the air in Earth's upper atmosphere a large amount of **friction** is created. Friction occurs when two objects rub together. Friction causes heat that could seriously damage a returning spacecraft. The American *Mercury* and the Soviet *Vostok* capsules were designed to deflect heat. Their shape, as well as their heat shields, helped protect the astronauts inside.

First Women in Space

The Soviet Union's Valentina Tereshkova was the first woman in space. She orbited Earth 48 times aboard the *Vostok 6* capsule in 1963. In 1983 the United States sent its first female astronaut, Sally Ride, into space. She was aboard the space shuttle *Challenger* and helped launch satellites into space.

friction · a force created when two objects rub together; friction slows down objects

Gary Powers (right) shows off a model of the U-2.

Spy in the Sky

U-2 Spy Plane

In May 1960 an American plane crashed in the Soviet Union and started an international dispute. What was American pilot Gary Powers doing 70,000 feet (21,336 m) over enemy territory? He was spying.

His plane, a top-secret U-2 spy plane, was created by the Central Intelligence Agency (CIA). The cameras on the plane were so advanced that they could take pictures of newspaper headlines from the sky. The U-2 was supposed to be undetectable in flight. However, the Soviets found it and shot it down. To keep enemies from learning U.S. secret technology, the spy plane was designed to self-destruct if it got shot down. Powers' plane did not self-destruct, and he survived the crash.

Powers was taken by the Soviets and sentenced to 10 years in prison. He was released a few weeks later. U.S. officials agreed to release a Soviet spy in their prison if Powers was let go. In the exchange, the spies were sent across opposite ends of a German bridge.

Spy Satellites

Since the 1950s countries have used spies on the ground, in the air, and even in space. Spy satellites have been secretly orbiting Earth for many years. Because they are so high above the surface, they are not easily detected or destroyed.

Some spy satellites are like giant cameras peering down at the planet. Their great height gives them a wide view of the planet below.

A U.S. satellite photo from 2002 shows an explosives factory in Iraq.

Powerful cameras can zoom in close enough to see enemy buildings and people on the ground. Some spy satellites are used to learn more about the land features of enemy territory.

Other spy satellites are used to listen to enemy communications. Signal satellites intercept, or interrupt, radio, telephone, and other transmissions. Some satellites have cameras and signal interceptors. This type of spy satellite helps countries see and hear their enemies.

Rockets launched a U.S. spy satellite into space in 2011.

Spy Photos

All satellites are launched into space by a rocket or a space shuttle. Once in space they move around Earth in an orbit. Over time, gravity slowly pulls them closer to Earth.

In the 1960s only government groups built satellites. Today, commercial companies with special skills build high-tech satellites and put them into orbit.

Spy satellites use digital cameras to take incredibly detailed pictures. The images are instantly sent to Earth through a wireless signal. Before there were digital cameras, some spy satellites took pictures using film. The film was actually shot back to Earth in special containers. U.S. Air Force crews had to snatch them out of the air over the Pacific Ocean. Once on the ground, the film was developed, and provided clues about enemy plans.

Top Secret Satellites

More than 1,000 working satellites may be currently orbiting Earth. The exact number is unknown. Many of these satellites are top secret.

Spy Drones

Remote-controlled flying robots called **drones** are popping up everywhere. Drones are robotic spies outfitted with cameras and microphones.

Drones come in many shapes and sizes. The U.S. Navy is developing some that are very tiny and look like insects. As planned, an insect drone will be able to fly up to a person and land. It will listen to and watch this person. The Navy is also developing drones that look like jellyfish. These "jellyfish" could be used by the Navy to spy on other ships.

Other types of drones look like airplanes and are just as big. These unmanned planes fly long missions over other countries to collect information. Scientists are working on new technology that will allow these supersecret spy planes to be recharged by lasers on the ground. Once this technology is perfected, the drones will never have to land to refuel.

drone · an unmanned aircraft

The MQ-1 Predator military drone spies on enemies.

Robots in Action

Scientists are building robots that can walk like humans and jump over high fences. Such robots could be used in war or in an urban setting. They could save lives by entering buildings and other areas that might be dangerous for humans.

Whether it's drones, satellites, or spy planes, the government has many ways to keep an eye on its enemies. Nobody knows for sure what the next big technology will be. There is one thing we can be sure of: The government's current plans are all top secret!

Eyes in the Sky

The Predator drone is also called a unmanned aerial vehicle, or UAV. UAVs keep track of enemy movements and send images back to the CIA.

Predator UAV

SATELLITE ANTENNA: THE SATELLITE ANTENNA IS INSIDE THE UAV'S NOSE. THE PILOT COMMANDS THE UAV USING SATELLITES WHEN THERE IS NO DIRECT LINK AVAILABLE.

NOSE CAMERA: THIS CAMERA BROADCASTS COLOR IMAGES TO HELP THE PILOT CONTROL THE UAV BY REMOTE CONTROL.

VARIABLE APERTURE CAMERAS: THESE ARE THE UAV'S MAIN EYES FOR SPYING. ONE OF THESE CAMERAS IS INFRARED. THE INFRARED CAMERA ALLOWS THE PREDATOR TO SEE IN THE DARK.

LENGTH: 27 FEET (8.2 METERS)

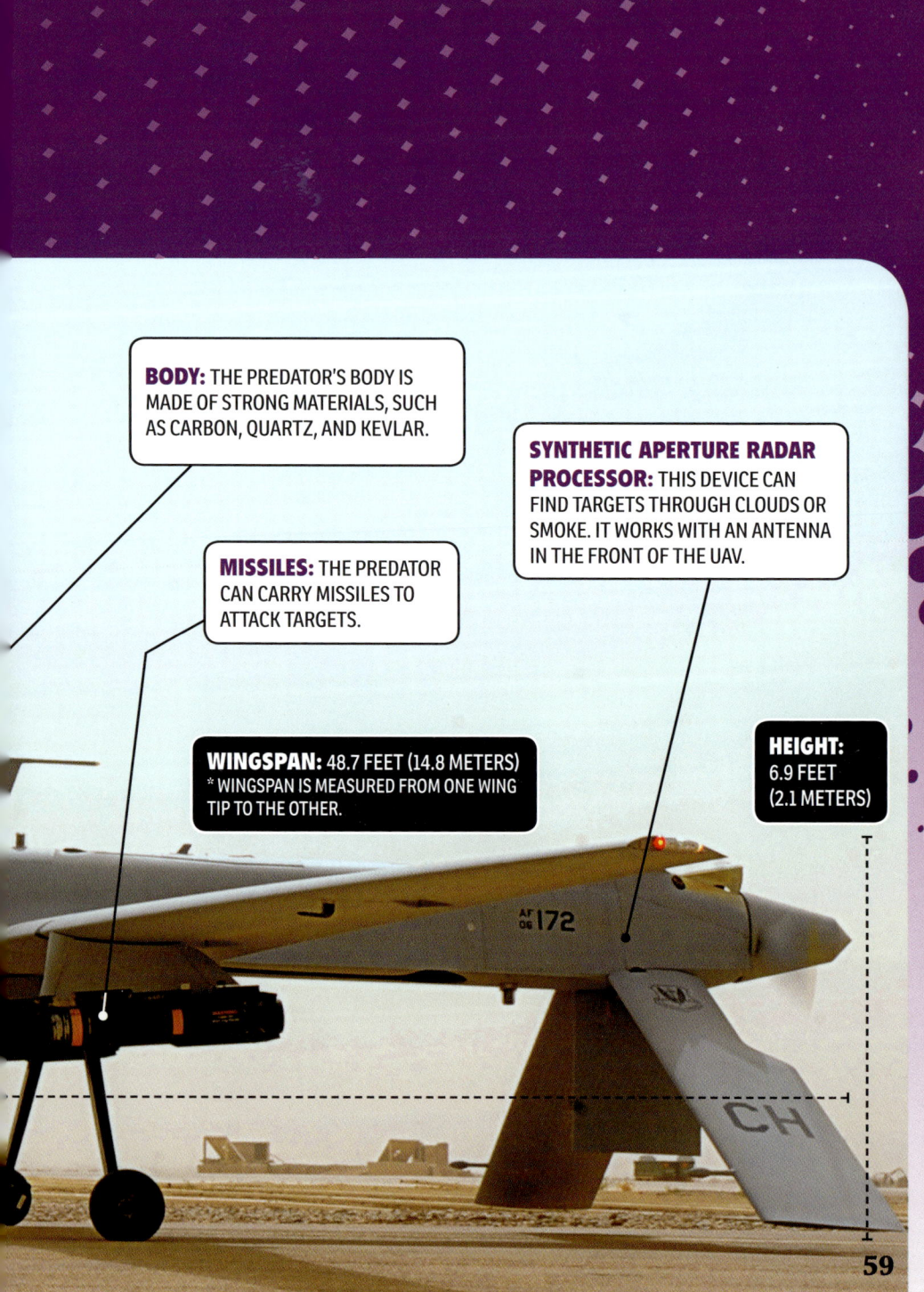

BODY: THE PREDATOR'S BODY IS MADE OF STRONG MATERIALS, SUCH AS CARBON, QUARTZ, AND KEVLAR.

SYNTHETIC APERTURE RADAR PROCESSOR: THIS DEVICE CAN FIND TARGETS THROUGH CLOUDS OR SMOKE. IT WORKS WITH AN ANTENNA IN THE FRONT OF THE UAV.

MISSILES: THE PREDATOR CAN CARRY MISSILES TO ATTACK TARGETS.

WINGSPAN: 48.7 FEET (14.8 METERS) * WINGSPAN IS MEASURED FROM ONE WING TIP TO THE OTHER.

HEIGHT: 6.9 FEET (2.1 METERS)

AF 06 172

CH

Read More

Hamilton, John. *B-2 Spirit Stealth Bomber*. Xtreme Military Aircraft. Minneapolis: ABDO Pub. Co., 2012.

Price, Sean Stewart. *World War II Spies*. Classified. North Mankato, Minn.: Capstone Press, 2014.

Rosinsky, Natalie. *The Story of the Atomic Bomb: How It Changed the World*. The World Transformed. Minneapolis: Compass Point Books, 2010.

Internet Sites

FactHound offers a safe, fun way to find Internet sites related to this book. All of the sites on FactHound have been researched by our staff.

Here's all you do:
Visit *www.facthound.com*
Type in this code: 9781625211002

Check out projects, games and lots more at
www.capstonekids.com

Glossary
of Text Features

Text Feature	How to Use it
Caption: A word or group of words shown with a picture or illustration	Read a caption to understand information that may not be in the text.
Diagram: A drawing that shows or explains something	Examine a diagram to understand steps in a process, how something is made, or the parts of something.
Glossary: List of key terms with their meanings	Look up key terms in the glossary to find their meanings and to get a better understanding of the topic of the text.
Index: Alphabetical list of key terms, names, and topics in a text with their page numbers	Use the index to find pages that contain information you are looking for.
Map: A drawing that represents a place, such as a country or city	Use a map to understand relative locations and determine where events took place.
Photograph or Illustration: Visuals that are created by cameras or drawn	Examine photographs and illustrations to better understand ideas in the text that might be unclear
Subhead: Word or group of words that divides the text into sections and tells the main idea of a section	Use subheads to locate information in the text and understand how a text is organized.
Table: Represents data in a small space	Examine a table to understand data or to compare information in the text.
Table of Contents: List of the major parts of the book and their page numbers	Use a table of contents to locate general information in the text and see how the topics are organized.
Text Box: A box in the text that provides extra information about a topic	Read a text box to understand interesting or important information.
Text Style: Bold, color, or italic words in the text	Pay attention to bold, italic, and color to figure out which words in the text are important words.
Timeline: Shows events in the order in which they occurred	Use a timeline to understand the order in which events occurred or how one event led to another.

Glossary

alliance (uh-LY-uhnts) · an agreement between nations or groups of people to work together

atmosphere (AT-muhss-fihr) · the mixture of gases that surrounds Earth

atomic bomb (uh-TAH-mik BOM) · a powerful explosive that destroys large areas; atomic bombs leave behind harmful energy called radiation

avatar (AV-uh-tahr) · a digital image that represents a person

biometrics (bahy-uh-ME-triks) · a system where a person's unique physical qualities are used to identify them

bunker (BUHNG-kuhr) · a strongly built room or building set beneath the ground to offer protection

capitalist (KA-puh-tuhl-ist) · having to do with supporting capitalism; capitalism is a way of organizing a country so that property is owned by individuals

capsule (KAP-suhl) · a sealed vehicle in which a person can ride in flight in space

communist (KAHM-yuh-nist) · having to do with supporting communism; communism is a way of organizing a country so that all the land, houses, and factories belong to the government or community

crater (KRAY-tuhr) · a large hole made by an object smashing into the ground

data (DAY-tuh) · information or facts

defensive weapons (di-FEN-siv WEP-uhns) · military weapons used for protection against an enemy

detonate (DET-en-ayt) · to cause something to explode

DNA profiling (dee-en-AY PROH-fuhy-ling) · the process of comparing DNA samples to determine if they are from the same person; DNA is the material in cells that gives people their individual characteristics; DNA stands for deoxyribonucleic acid

drone (DROHN) · an unmanned aircraft

element (E-luh-muhnt) · a substance made of atoms that cannot be broken down into simpler substances

enrich (in-RICH) · to improve